MALCOLM THE POO

By

Simon Hucknall

For
Vicki and Jess
The most amazing, talented, brave and beautiful
wife and daughter a chap could wish for.

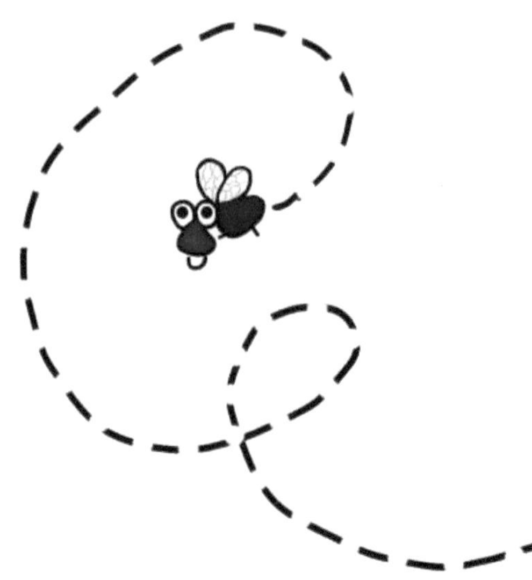

First published in 2023 United Kingdom
Jesivi Publishing
Copyright © Simon Hucknall
sihucknall@gmail.com

ISBN
978-1-3999-7434-9

Malcolm wasn't happy because Malcolm was a poo.
Hiya
He was small and brown and smelly and unsure what to do.

He had fallen from the bottom of a fine old horse named Jack.
Why did the bakers hands smell?
COME BACK MUM,,,

Who trotted off without a second thought and never once looked back.

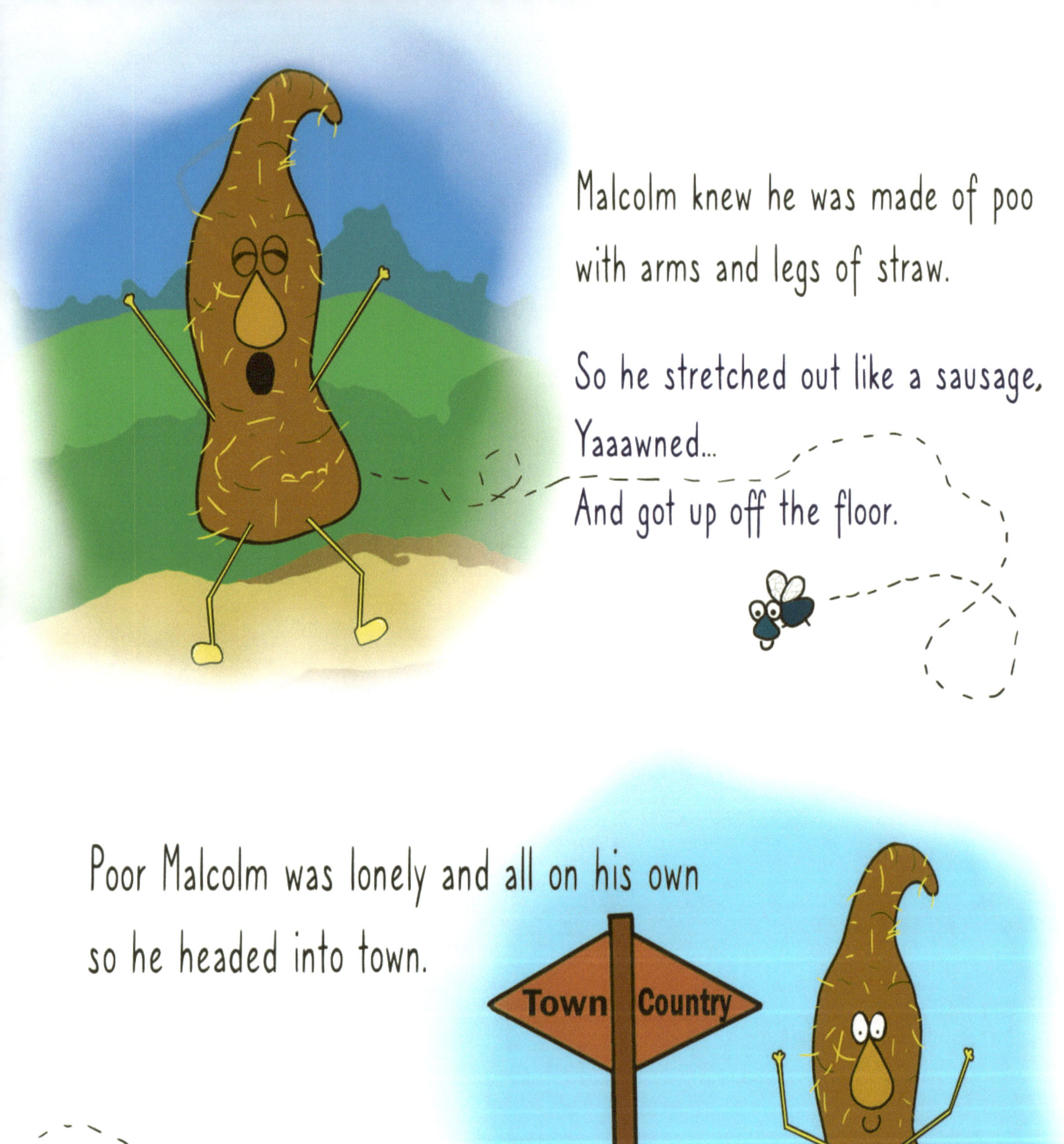

Malcolm knew he was made of poo
with arms and legs of straw.

So he stretched out like a sausage,
Yaaawned...
And got up off the floor.

Poor Malcolm was lonely and all on his own
so he headed into town.

But everyone he smiled at responded with a frown.
Did that poo just smile at me.

Malcolm followed fashion
to look like other guys.

But it's not easy looking cool and hip
when you're attracting flies.

What's it called when
you pretend to use the
toilet?

A sham poo

POO'S
NBR
1

Can I come in?

So our Malcolm tried to make new friends
and fit in with the crowd.

But everywhere the same four words
sorry NO POOS ALLOWED.

He wasn't good at parties
he could not dance or sing.

He just sat there in the corner
leaving stains on everything.

He tried.....

Rodeo.....
Did you hear about the man who sat under a cow
He got a pat on the head

Ski jumping....
What would Malcolm look at through a telescope?
The pooniverse.

Even surfing at the beach.

But everywhere that poor Malc went
IT'S POO!
He'd hear them mutter.

So one day Malcolm just gave up
and lay down in the gutter.

Now there was a man, a gardener,
who's name was Mr Barrett.
VEG SHOW
Winner
Best
Carrott
1
every year he tried to win the cup for
BIGGEST,
FATTEST,
carrot.

But this year's was not up to scratch
and way too small to show.
Mr Barrett had tried everything
to get the lad to grow.

He tried....

Reading him books.

Dropping beats.

Even taking him to the fair.

But carrot just sat there looking bored and not growing
and didn't seem to care.

So feeling low and out of luck
Mr Barrett thought, what can I do?
Then like a blinding flash he had an idea
"EUREKA" he cried
"I need POO"

So he tugged on his boots and pulled on his coat
and went out searching for poo.

Then after a while he looked down in the gutter
and spotted. Can you guess who?

IT WAS MALCOLM!
YES MALCOLM!
OUR MALCOLM!
THE POO!!!

"You're a fine fellow", said old Mr Barrett.
"I'll take you to my greenhouse
and spread you on my carrot."

"WAHOO MALCOLM IS BACK.
DO YOU THINK HE LOOKS TIRED?"
"HE DOES LOOK
A LITTLE POOPED."

So then Malcolm was happy
and felt useful too.
But poor carrot was upset
because he now smelt like poo.

But as the days past by old Barrett knew,
his idea had been a good one because carrot grew...

And grew...

Day of the big veg show.

And grew...

VILLAGE
AND GREW.

So on the day of the veg show
they knew that greatness beckoned...

But did they win the big fine cup?

No...

I'm sorry to say they came second.

Although Malcolm and carrot were dissapointed
Mr Barrett was without a care.

"Don't worry lads" he said with a smile.
"We'll try again next year".

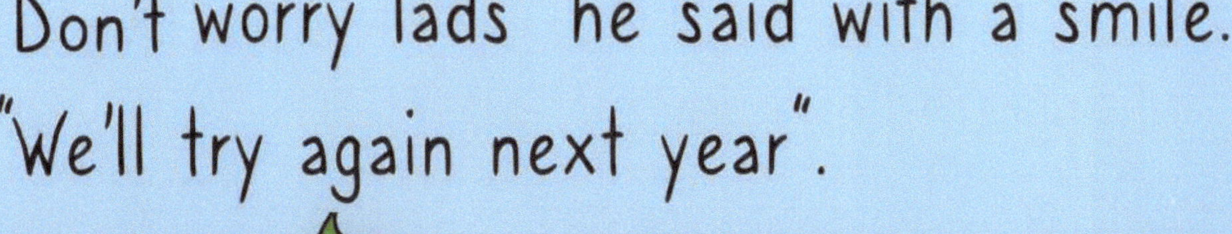

So the moral of our tale is that we all have different skills,
things that we enjoy that make us happy and fulfilled.

It may be football or tennis or netball or darts.
Or reading and writing, maths, science, or art.

Using computers or playing guitar, riding a bike or looking at stars..
Dancing or singing or making up jokes,
running and jumping or climbing up ropes.

Walking up mountains or parachuting from planes,
the possibilities are endless
so all that remains...

Is to say...

Find something that's rewarding and really fun to do, there's something for everyone,

IT'S ALL UP TO YOU!

It's trying thats important, and we may not always win. If at first we don't succeed, we must *try* and *try* again.

Everyone is special, we all have things that we can do.

Everyone has purpose......

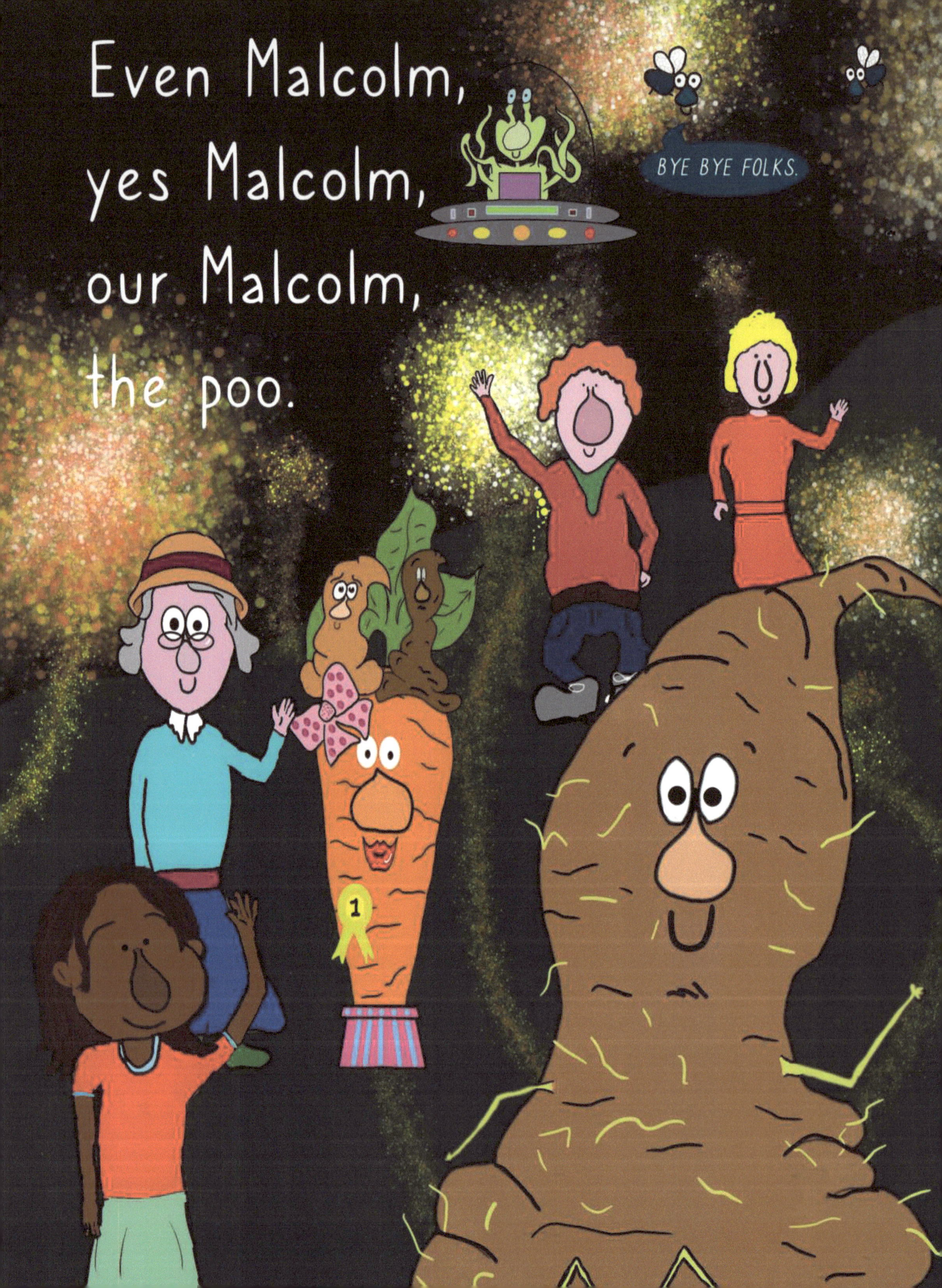
Even Malcolm,
yes Malcolm,
our Malcolm,
the poo.
BYE BYE FOLKS.

THE END.